A PRACTICAL
GUIDE TO
EFFECTIVE
LISTENING

A PRACTICAL GUIDE TO EFFECTIVE LISTENING

Diane Bone

KOGAN
PAGE

First published in the United States of America in 1988 by Crisp Publications Inc, 95 First Street, Los Altos, California 94022, USA

This edition first published in Great Britain in 1988 by Kogan Page Ltd, 120 Pentonville Road, London N1 9JN

British Library Cataloguing in Publication Data

Bone, Diane
    A practical guide to effective listening.
    1. Business firms. Personnel. Inter-
    personal relationships. Listening
    I. Title   II. Series
    650.1'3

    ISBN 1-85091-785-X
    ISBN 1-85091-786-8 Pbk

Typeset by the Castlefield Press, Wellingborough
Printed and bound in Great Britain by
Dotesios (Printers) Ltd, Bradford-on-Avon, Wiltshire

Contents

Preface   7

The Business of Listening   9

Some Important Objectives for the Reader   10

1. Why Should You (or Anyone) Listen?   11
   What's in it for me? *11*
   The benefits of listening – a quiz *12*
   Asleep at the switch: the costs of lazy listening *13*
   Why should we listen? *15*
   Fifty reasons to become a better listener *16*
   The joy of small change *17*

2. Four Key Elements of Good Listening   18
   How to be a good listener *18*
   1. Hear the message *18*
   2. Accurately interpret the speaker's message *21*
   3. Evaluate the message *24*
   4. Respond to the message *25*

3. Your Listening Style – a Barrier or a Bridge?   27
   Barriers to communication *27*
   Bridges to communication *29*

4. How Well Do You Listen?   32
   A listening attitude: your key to success *32*

Personal listening inventory 34
Your listening qualities: an awareness exercise 36
How to stop bad listening habits 37

5. **Ten Tips for Tip-Top Listening**   **39**
   1. Take notes 39
   2. Listen now, report later 40
   3. Learn to want to listen 41
   4. Be present 43
   5. Anticipate excellence 45
   6. Become a 'whole body' listener 46
   7. Build rapport by pacing the speaker 48
   8. Control your emotional 'hot buttons' 51
   9. Control distractions 54
   10. Listening is a gift, give generously 56

6. **Summary: Points to Remember**   **57**
   Summary 57
   Develop a personal action plan 58
   Kathy's story 59

Further Reading from Kogan Page   **61**

Preface

If you want to improve your ability to listen effectively in your business and personal life, this book is for you. Most of us are not good listeners. While at work, we normally listen at about 25 per cent of our listening capacity. Most of us *think* we are good listeners, and that overconfidence may be the reason for our downfall. Even if we devote full concentration to listening we cannot listen at 100 per cent efficiency for very long. And at 100 per cent efficiency, the message we are listening to must be important enough to sustain our attention.

Humans listen more than anything else, except breathe. Carefully reading this book will help you learn to listen better, on the job and at home. Before good listening can happen you must *want* to be a good listener. Whether you are a secretary, an account executive, a programmer or a project manager, you can improve your listening if you have the desire, the interest, a high level of concentration, self-discipline and a positive attitude.

This book will provide you with important listening know-how. It is a self-study introduction to the basic skills you need to become a better listener. It will provide many helpful suggestions for incorporating more effective listening skills into your business day. Listening styles and motivation are highly individual, so there is no claim as to how much your listening skills will improve. We offer many suggestions for improvement, along with some motivation to help you make constructive changes in your listening style. After completing *A Practical Guide to Effective Listening* you can practise your new-found listening awareness on business associates, family and friends.

Each part of this book provides insights, useful tips and practical guidelines for upgrading your skills. These are the *why*, *what*, and *how* of listening. Each part contains activities called 'Listening Labs' as well as case studies and checklists. They provide 'hands on' reinforcements and illustrations for the key principles of the book.

Chapter 1 provides answers to the important question, 'Why should I become a better listener?'

Chapter 2 describes how good listeners process information and reach higher levels of listening expertise.

In *Chapter 3* individual listening styles are identified as barriers or bridges to communication.

Chapter 4 contains pencil exercises to help you define your listening strengths and weaknesses.

Chapter 5 provides ten tips to reinforce your listening strengths, control your weaknesses, and reach new levels of listening effectiveness.

Chapter 6 provides a summary of the main points.

Plan to find three ideas from this book to begin practising immediately. Use this practical guide as a reference and challenge yourself to practise until you have mastered each new skill. Remember: practice, properly done, does not make perfect, it makes permanent. Listening well will help you to function more effectively in both your business *and* personal life. So pick up your pencil, tune up your ears, and turn to Chapter 1.

Diane Bone

The Business of Listening

In Business . . .

To listen effectively is to reach a clarity of understanding
To understand clearly is to respond appropriately
To respond appropriately is to enhance communication
To enhance communication is to support cooperation
To support cooperation is to improve morale
To improve morale is to increase job commitment
To increase job commitment is to focus on productivity
Listening is good business.

Some Important Objectives
for the Reader

Objectives give us a sense of direction, a definition of what we plan to accomplish, and a sense of fulfilment when they are achieved. Tick the objectives that are important to you. This book will help you achieve them.

By completing this book, I plan to:

☐ Learn the basics of effective listening skills.
☐ Learn to recognise good listening behaviour and incorporate it into my daily activities.
☐ Understand the impact of good listening skills on productivity.
☐ Learn to correct problems caused by poor listening habits and systematically change them into permanent good habits.

CHAPTER 1
Why Should You (or Anyone) Listen?

What's in it for me?

At least half of all communication time is spent listening. Experts in a dozen studies have verified that more than any other activity, except breathing, we listen. Listening is the 'receiving' part of communication. Listening is:

1. Receiving information through your ears (and eyes);
2. Giving meaning to that information;
3. Deciding what you think (or feel) about that information; and
4. Responding to what you hear.

Much of our listening is work related. We spend countless hours of our working life involved in listening-related activities. The following is a partial list of work-related activities which involve listening. Tick those which apply to you.

☐ Attending meetings, briefings and lectures
☐ Personal counselling (one-to-one)
☐ Giving instructions
☐ Receiving instructions
☐ Interviewing others
☐ Making decisions based on verbal information
☐ Selling or marketing a product or service
☐ Managing others
☐ Helping clients
☐ Servicing other groups or departments
☐ Using the telephone.

If you are like most people, you ticked most of the activities on the previous page. What other work-related activities can you think of that involve listening?

_____

_____

_____

_____

_____

What is the business of listening? More important, what's in it for you? Tick those items with which you agree:

Listening effectively can:
☐ Increase your income.
☐ Improve your company's profits.
☐ Make you more promotable.
☐ Increase your job satisfaction.
☐ Improve your ability to solve problems.
☐ Keep you aware of what is going on in your organisation.

The benefits of listening – a quiz

Read each of the following statements. Decide which are true and which false about the benefits that good listening can bring in business relationships. Check your answers with those of the author at the bottom of page 13.

True or false

_____ 1. Skill in listening improves your self-confidence.

_____ 2. People like you when you listen to them.

_____ 3. Good listeners are usually more efficient in completing their work.

_____ 4. What you create with good listening is flexibility in settling disagreements.

_____ 5. Intelligent responses are easier when you listen.

_____ 6. More decisions are made by 'shooting from the hip' than by listening to the opinions of others.

_____ 7. Learning to listen to clients helps you to respond more quickly to their needs.

_____ 8. Few good listeners are promoted to top management positions.

_____ 9. Good listeners are not often embarrassed by unnecessary mistakes.

_____ 10. Handling distractions is difficult for good listeners.

Organisations rely heavily upon listening as an important productivity tool. They need people who have good listening communication skills. Those who know how to listen can:

- Better understand problems
- Sustain attention
- Retain information
- Improve working relationships.

Business thrives when employees listen.

Asleep at the switch: the costs of lazy listening

Most of us are not good listeners. We listen at about 25 per cent of our potential, which means we _ignore, forget, distort_ or _misunderstand_ 75 per cent of what we hear. Hard to believe, perhaps, but true. Such lazy listening habits can be very costly, both to our business and to ourselves.

Answers
1.T 2.T 3.T 4.T 5.T 6.F (Committees, meetings and informal networks are strong evidence that most decisions are made by groups.) 7.T 8.F (Most surveys rank listening as one of the three most important skills of top managers.) 9.T 10.F (Good listeners know how to control distractions by eliminating or ignoring them.)

Paul Leet of the Sperry Corporation has stated: 'Poor listening is one of the most significant problems facing business today. Business relies on clear communication. When communication breaks down, costly mistakes are made. Organisations pay for mistakes caused by poor listening with lower profits, and customers pay for the same mistakes with higher prices.'

Lazy listening is a hidden cost of doing business. Suppose you were employed by a large international company with 10,000 employees. If each person in the company made one £50 error each year because of poor listening, the company would lose half a million pounds. This loss would be especially bad news if your company had a profit sharing plan or was forced to lay off workers due to poor earnings.

The following examples highlight the costs of lazy listening.

Case 1
A sales manager for a large company asked his accounts department how he could charge off a £10,000 error caused by a despatcher who routed a fleet of drivers to deliver building materials to the wrong county. The despatcher heard the first part of the town (Newcastle) but did not wait for the rest. The consignment went to Newcastle upon Tyne instead of Newcastle-under-Lyme. How could this problem have been avoided?

Case 2
Three computer sales representatives from different companies presented their products to a historian who had special application needs. The historian was a dealer in rare manuscripts and explained to each sales representative what computer functions were required. Two of the sales representatives did not listen and presented products that were inappropriate. The third understood what the historian wanted and she got the order. The manuscript dealer was impressed with only one thing, and it wasn't the hardware because he didn't know much about computers. He did know that two people didn't listen and the third did. He bought his computer from the person who listened. What was the cost to the other two companies?

Case 3

Linda recently cut short a business trip to attend an important investment dinner meeting with her husband. She hurried from the airport, dressed for dinner and met her husband at the restaurant. An hour and a half later their financial adviser had not arrived. A phone call established they were at the right restaurant, but on the wrong night. The dinner was rebooked, but Linda sacrificed profitable business she would have closed had she kept to her original itinerary. How can Linda avoid this problem in the future?

Why should we listen?

Why should we listen? What are the advantages of overcoming lazy listening habits and changing unproductive ways of listening? List as many reasons as you can think of in the space below. Place a ☑ next to those that are most important to you. Then turn the page and read 'Fifty reasons to become a better listener'. Tick any you would like to add to your list.

Reasons for me to become a better listener

Fifty reasons to become a better listener

1. To learn something
2. To be entertained
3. To understand a situation
4. To get information
5. To be courteous
6. To be responsible
7. To prevent accidents
8. To be a team player
9. To ask intelligent questions
10. To improve confidence
11. To protect freedom
12. To find out people's needs
13. To reach a productivity or sales quota
14. To be valued and trusted
15. To use money wisely
16. To be more efficient
17. To make accurate evaluations
18. To make comparisons
19. To understand and be understood
20. To analyse the speaker's purpose
21. To develop a reputation for being a good listener
22. To get the best value
23. To improve discipline
24. To enhance relationships
25. To solve problems
26. To show you care
27. To satisfy curiosity
28. To be safe
29. To be a good lover
30. To make intelligent decisions
31. To prevent waste
32. To make money
33. To avoid embarrassment
34. To stay out of trouble
35. To save time
36. To be a discriminating consumer
37. To be a supportive friend
38. To give an appropriate response

39. To enjoy the sounds of nature
40. To create win-win situations
41. To control distractions
42. To increase concentration
43. To improve your vocabulary
44. To build rapport
45. To be prepared for sudden shifts in a speaker's topic or intention
46. To be a better family member
47. To settle disagreements
48. To maintain a flexible attitude
49. To improve your personality
50. To use the gift of hearing.

The joy of small change

To improve the listening skills suggested in this book, we must be both motivated and educated. We must believe that each small change in lazy listening habits has value for us.

Change can be hard work. Setbacks sometimes occur just when we think we're making progress. To change our listening habits we must believe that the new skills we are gaining are worth the unproductive habits we are giving up. As you change your behaviour to practise listening techniques presented in the pages ahead, the following suggestions will be helpful. To change effectively, it is recommended that you:

1. *Notice small changes.* Recognise your improvements and give yourself a pat on the back as they occur. Acknowledging improvements is a form of positive reinforcement.
2. *Keep a log of significant listening habit changes,* such as:
   - Enjoying a previously dull meeting.
   - Receiving positive responses from others.
   - Feeling good about not interrupting a colleague at coffee.
3. *Acknowledge setbacks but do not give in to them.* Failure to learn from mistakes is the only real failure.
4. *Stay with it.* Unless you consciously work to improve your listening skills, you will find it easy to slip back into old (bad) habits.

CHAPTER 2
Four Key Elements of Good Listening

How to be a good listener

Good listening is an active, integrated communication skill that demands energy and know-how. It is purposeful, powerful and productive. To listen effectively we must *hear* and *select* information from the speaker, *give it meaning, decide how we feel about it,* and *respond* – in a matter of seconds!

We must also understand the speaker's purpose in order to know how to listen most effectively. The speaker's purpose influences the way we listen and how we perceive what is said. The speaker and the listener must have the same purpose if communication is to be effective. Next time you are listening to someone, make sure you are aware what that person's purpose is. Is he or she:

- Entertaining you?
- Providing critical data?
- Persuading you?
- Sharing feelings?
- Making small talk?

On the following pages are the four key elements of the listening process. They describe what good listeners do to listen more effectively. After each element is a 'Listening Lab' that contains suggestions and exercises to improve your listening skills.

1. Hear the message

Our brain recognises sound as it enters the ear. Other

'listening channels' such as our eyes and our feelings seek confirmation of the message from the speaker's non-verbal feedback (body language) and tone of voice. Hearing is the *beginning* of the listening process. It is non-selective and involuntary. However, when you *choose* to listen, it is on purpose.

Listening is voluntary

From the constant noise around us, we select what we want to listen to. This information moves from short-term memory (STM) to long-term memory (LTM). Short-term memory is a 'holding pen' for incoming signals from our five senses. To protect us from too much stimulation, STM has a limited capacity and is easily disrupted. For instance, a mail clerk would not be likely retain much information from a technical discussion about Data Transport Protocols because he/she would have no use for the message. The information would probably be held in STM for 1–30 seconds and then dismissed. If the information we hear is not recognised and selected for processing, it is dismissed from STM.

In a sense, we are pre-programmed. Our choices of what to listen to come from previous choices based on interests and needs. John enjoys investing in stocks and shares, so he always has his 'ears open' for tips on the market. Ellie 'tunes in' whenever someone is discussing consumer rights. Ralph 'catches' the football scores each Saturday to track his favourite teams. In other words, we choose what we want to listen to and it is often based on our past choices.

In order to listen to a speaker, we begin by *hearing* and *selecting* (paying attention to) oral messages, and accompanying non-verbal signals. When these messages are interesting or important, we pay attention to them.

We choose to listen because:

- The message is important;
- We are interested;
- We feel like listening; or
- We listened to this kind of information in the past.

Sometimes, even when we choose to listen, anger, frustration, grief or hostility can act as 'emotional cotton wool' in our ears. We tend to hear what we expect (or want) to hear, and filter out that which is not consistent with our feelings and attitudes. For example, Jennifer was on her way to lunch when her manager dropped a report on her desk and said he needed 20 sets of copies when he returned from lunch. Jennifer was upset because her friends were waiting and she assumed she had to make the copies. She did not hear her boss say after *his* lunch, which was an hour later than hers. She would have had ample time to make the copies after she returned from her lunch had she listened carefully.

Three keys to hearing the message
- Pay attention
- Select what is important
- Recognise emotional messages

Listening lab for key element 1 – Hear the message

Exercise 1
Sit quietly in a place where people are talking around you (hotel lounge, office corridor, restaurant, airport). Listen for about ten minutes and then write down what you heard, ie, what people said, and other incidental sounds or noises. This activity should make you conscious of the many voices and sounds that bombard you daily. It should help to remind you that listening begins with hearing but is a voluntary activity.

1. What did you hear?
2. How many sounds do you remember?
3. What sounds did you remember most easily?
4. Did your mind wander while you were listening?
5. Try the experiment again with your eyes closed and see if the results are the same. (You will notice how important your eyes are to listening.)

Author's comments
1. We hear sounds constantly, but remember few. 2. We remember sounds that are important, interesting or unusual. 3. Same as 2. 4. All of us daydream frequently. We cannot remember what we did not hear. 5. People sometimes complain that they can't hear as well when they are not wearing glasses because they cannot see speaker's non-verbal message.

Exercise 2
Listed below are some methods for improving listening at the 'hearing' level. Write down any others you can think of.

- Improve your listening vocabulary so that words and meanings are clear when you listen.
- Have your hearing checked.
- Ask for repetition or clarification.
- Overcome the tendency to daydream.
- Eliminate distractions.

Others

- _____

- _____

- _____

- _____

- _____

2. Accurately interpret the speaker's message

Interpreting a speaker's message is coming to a mutual understanding of the speaker's meaning. Good listeners know that a match in meaning is a match in understanding. The word communication comes from the Latin root word *communis* which means 'common', a common or shared understanding.

Listeners often experience problems at the interpreting level because no two people perceive things in the same way. Speakers do not always say exactly what they mean, or mean exactly what they say.

WHAT IS THE DIFFERENCE?
'When I look at you, time stands still.'
'You have a face that would stop a clock.'

'We probably do not interpret accurately in most listening situations. Listening is a complicated process. Speakers send messages to listeners both verbally and non-verbally. If Jim tells Rod, 'You have to do something about the Doughty account,' Rod must assign meaning to Jim's *words*, *filters*, *tone of voice*, and *non-verbal cues*.

Words. Words are merely vehicles for the thoughts and feelings of the speaker. Words are not actual experiences, but a means of explaining experiences. It is people who give meaning to words.

Filters. Both listeners and speakers have filters which can help or hinder the interpreting process. These filters are in our brain's 'database' and attach personal meaning to information as it is presented. Some examples of filters include the following. Can you add others?

memories	values
perceptions	knowledge and intelligence
biases	feelings
attitudes	language and vocabulary
expectations	needs and motives
emotional triggers	age
current attention span	sensory acuity
past experiences	assumptions

Tone of voice. Most voices convey approximately 30 per cent of the meaning of a message. Voices can be insistent, pleading, questioning, whining, demanding, etc. Tom speaks in a quiet monotone. Even though he is intelligent, his voice lacks conviction, and people don't take him seriously. What could Tom do with his voice to make people listen to him?

Non-verbal cues. A non-verbal cue, or body language, is a message sent by such things as a speaker's gestures, facial expressions, eyes and posture. Good listeners use their ears, eyes and intuition to interpret a speaker's non-verbal feedback. Non-verbal cues confirm or deny the message of the words and tones of voice. More than half of most human interaction is through non-verbal communication.

Good listeners who aren't sure of the speaker's meaning will ask for repetition or clarification (feedback).

'Is this what you meant when you say . . . ?'

'This is how I interpret what you are saying . . . Am I correct?'

'I'm not sure I understand your meaning; could you be more specific?'

Three keys to interpreting the message
- Self-knowledge
- Desire to understand
- Asking for clarification

Listening lab for key element 2 – Interpret the message

Let us imagine you have just interviewed a young woman for an important sales position in your department. As she is leaving she remembers one last thing she wants you to know, and states: 'By the way, I was in the top 10 per cent of my college year.' She then shakes your hand, thanks you for the interview and leaves. How would you interpret her statement? 'The following are some possible interpretations. Read these, then list five other possible interpretations of her statement.

'By the way, I was in the top 10 per cent of my college year.'

1. She is intelligent.
2. She is competitive.
3. The college was not academically challenging.
4. She studied constantly.
5. She was bragging.
6. _____
7. _____
8. _____
9. _____
10. _____

How would you clarify your interpretation?

See the author's comments below.

Comments. Good listeners want to understand the speaker's meaning. They are aware of their own filters and those of the speaker, and they *ask questions* if they need clarification.

3. Evaluate the message

Good listeners make sure they have all the key information before forming an opinion. They do not jump to conclusions based on a bias or incomplete information. They may agree or disagree with the speaker. Good listening does not mean automatic compliance. A good listener will weigh and analyse all the evidence before reaching a final decision or making a written or verbal judgement.

Diana is a member of a jury trying a larceny case. As each counsel sifts through the evidence Diana listens carefully for validation of her opinions. She is careful not to jump to conclusions based on emotional testimony. At the conclusion of the trial Diana evaluates all the evidence presented by both sides before making a statement about her decision. The jury foreman later thanked Diana for her valuable observations and objective comments.

We make conscientious evaluations when we make decisions based on *all* the available information. We run into problems with evaluation when we think mechanically, or jump to conclusions. We must ask ourselves if we are listening *to* someone or listening *against* them. Are we *evaluating* or making a *value judgement*?

Evaluation is not required in every listening situation; therefore, we must also know our purpose for listening.

Three keys to evaluating the message
- Ask questions
- Analyse the evidence
- Don't jump to conclusions

Listening lab for key element 3 – Evaluate the message
We listen constantly to advertising on radio and television. How often do you stop to evaluate the slant or bias of advertisers who want us to buy their services or products? How often do you ask if the information is reasonable and

logical? The following description of Adolph Hitler could have been written by his press agent. Read the description as if you were listening to it, taking note of the press agent's built-in bias. Then answer the questions that follow.

Our leader had an unhappy childhood and little formal education. His father bitterly opposed his ambition to become an artist. Through self-education, he became the author of a book that became a national bestseller. Obstacles do not discourage him. When others say, 'That is not possible,' he hurdles each barrier as it comes. He has built an active youth movement of selected young people. He is known throughout the world for his dynamic speeches. His closest associates say of him, 'He accomplishes great deeds out of the passion of his will in order to create the kind of government he believes in.'

1. How would you evaluate Hitler if you had not heard of him before you read this description?
2. Are any character flaws suggested in the description?
3. What suggestions does the press agent use to create a positive impression of Hitler?
4. How can this exercise help you to evaluate information more carefully?

4. Respond to the message

Although a response may be considered a speaking rather than a listening role, it is critical to clear communication. The listener must let the speaker know by verbal and/or non-verbal feedback what was heard and how it was heard. Good listeners accept responsibility to provide feedback to the speaker in order to complete the communication process.

Good listeners have a strong desire to reach a common understanding. Responsible responses inform the speaker that:

1. The message was heard.
2. It was understood.
3. It was evaluated appropriately.

Several problems can occur in this key element. One is when no response occurs. If Karla asks Jack when the plans for the new office building will be available, and Jack simply looks at Karla without indicating that he heard her, he is not communicating effectively. Although silence can communicate, a blank stare is not a responsible response. Other problems include responses that are defensive, overly emotional, or inappropriate. If Jack had abruptly changed the subject, his response would have also been inappropriate. Finally, a confusing response (ie, a double message) can occur when the verbal (words and tone of voice) and non-verbal (actions and body language) elements are in conflict.

Three keys to responding to the message
- Want to reach a common understanding
- Give feedback verbally and/or non-verbally
- Avoid confusing messages

Listening lab for key element 4 – Respond to the message
The following are several possible responses in listening situations. Tick those you think are important for good communication.

☐ Providing prompt feedback.
☐ Giving feedback that is relevant to the conversation.
☐ Changing the subject.
☐ Interrupting by waving your arms or stamping your feet.
☐ Using appropriate eye contact.
☐ Combining verbal and non-verbal (body language) feedback for more complete communication.
☐ Staring blankly.
☐ Asking a question for clarification.
☐ Mumbling.

Add your own responsible responses below:

CHAPTER 3
Your Listening Style – A Barrier or a Bridge?

Listening style reflects the attitude and behaviour of the listener. It is how an individual responds when listening. Your listening style can be a *bridge* or a *barrier* to good communication. Listeners can avoid the barriers of listening by being aware of what the pitfalls are, and knowing how to avoid them.

Some descriptions of listening styles are given below. Answer the questions following each description which help these 'characters' to improve their listening styles.

Barriers to communication

Vacant Vincent

The most difficult person to communicate with is a daydreamer. Meet Vacant Vincent. You will recognise him by the far-away look in his eyes. Vincent is like a social butterfly who dips in and out of conversations picking up bits and pieces of information. He is physically present but 'not really there'. Vincent is easily distracted, and often changes the subject without warning. Sometimes he slouches as if the is tired. He plays with his tie or impatiently taps his pencil on the desk. The best way to get Vincent's attention is to talk about *his* interests.

How can Vincent become a better listener? Tick any of the following that would help Vincent to improve his communication skills.

1. ☐ Sitting in a listening position
2. ☐ Making eye contact
3. ☐ Controlling distractions
4. ☐ Playing with his computer
5. ☐ Fidgeting
6. ☐ Sticking to the subject
7. ☐ Taking an interest in other people
8. ☐ Losing his temper

Critical Carrie

Critical listening is important in business, especially when problems need to be resolved, but some listeners listen only to find fault. Critical Carrie listens to get all the facts, but is so critical of each item that she often misses 'the big picture'. Carrie frowns or rolls her eyes in disbelief as she listens to elements of a problem. Her questions for clarification are demanding and make her colleagues feel cornered. Critical Carrie is an incessant note-taker, so her eye contact is limited. She finds little time for small talk. Her friends wish she would 'lighten up' and not take things so seriously.

What would help Carrie to communicate more effectively? Tick any of the following that would help Carrie improve her listening style.

1. ☐ Building rapport with small talk
2. ☐ Listening for the 'big picture'
3. ☐ Taking more notes
4. ☐ Becoming a better friend to herself
5. ☐ Discrediting the speaker
6. ☐ Deciding the purpose of the discussion
7. ☐ Developing patience
8. ☐ Jumping to conclusions

Answers to Critical Carrie
1, 2, 4, 6, 7.

Answers to Vacant Vincent
1, 2, 3, 6, 7.

Compliant Curtis

Compliant listening is passive behaviour that does not allow the speaker to understand the real feelings or opinions of the listener. Listeners such as compliant Curtis listen more than they talk. Often they are shy. They want to please others and keep communication pleasant. Compulsive talkers often seek out listeners like compliant Curtis because they need people with the patience to listen to them. Unfortunately, when Curtis speaks he usually keeps his *real* opinions to himself for fear of criticism. Sometimes he fakes attention as he silently thinks his private thoughts. In meetings Curtis nods his head approvingly, but adds little to the discussion. You will recognise compliant Curtis by such phrases as 'That's nice', or 'I see your point'.

How can Curtis become a more involved listener? Tick any of the following actions that would help him to improve his listening style.

1. ☐ Voicing his opinions
2. ☐ Working to develop positive assertiveness
3. ☐ Daydreaming
4. ☐ Asking questions
5. ☐ Listening more intently
6. ☐ Mentally finishing other people's sentances
7. ☐ Speaking with conviction
8. ☐ Avoiding eye contact

Bridges to communication

'Active' listening is the bridge to good communication. It is committed listening based on good habits and self-control. Good listening is purposeful and productive because it allows the listener and the speaker to reach understanding. Descriptions of active listening styles that create positive communication are given on the next page.

Answers to Compliant Curtis
1, 2, 4, 6, 7.

Active Alan

Active Alan, a skilled training director, is an involved listener. He is 'present' and participative and assumes responsibility for the success of communications in his department. In meetings and discussions Alan requires discipline and relevance from his subordinates and bridges gaps in understanding by asking questions for clarification. Individuals in his department appreciate Alan's clear verbal *and* non-verbal responses and focused eye contact. Alan tries to see the other person's point of view and refrains from evaluating information too quickly. As an active listener, Alan listens not only to the *content* of employees' statements, but also to their *intent*.

Listening Lisette

Listening Lisette, a successful estate agent, credits her success to active listening. When interviewing potential clients, Lisette listens carefully to their requirements for a home. She pays close attention to where they want to live, the desired style of house and the value they place on schools and services. She asks many questions for clarification. She then 'feeds back' what she hears to be sure she is accurate in her interpretation. By the end of a busy 'listening' day, Lisette often feels as tired as if she had built a house, rather than sold one. She realises that active listening is hard work but knows her results are measured clearly by her commissions, her satisfied new home owners, and new friends she makes because she helped them with a major decision.

What other listening styles (positive and negative) can you think of?

Listening styles	Style	Attitude Conveyed	Verbal or non-verbal behaviour
Positive Negative			

CHAPTER 4

How Well Do You Listen?

A listening attitude: your key to success

What kind of a listener are you? Conscientious? Rushed? Thoughtful? Interruptive? This section provides you with some methods for self-evaluation as a listener. What is your listening style? How well does it contribute to your overall success in business? In your personal life?

Most people believe they are effective listeners. However, as previously noted, research indicates that on average we are effective and listen at only a 25 per cent efficiency level. Much of the time we *think* we are listening. We seem to believe that because we have ears we are listening. This is like believing that because we have eyes we can read. Undiagnosed bad habits such as interrupting, allowing ourselves to be distracted, jumping to conclusions, daydreaming or giving in to boredom prevent us from becoming the kind of listeners we think we are. The only way for us to progress is to make some conscious changes.

Change begins with an honest self-evaluation of our strengths *and* weaknesses. The exercises that follow will allow you to evaluate your listening style and plan a strategy for change.

Practising the exercises will make you a better listener. First, identify your listening problems and decide which changes you want to make. To be effective, plan positive action steps, and then practise specific listening skills at every opportunity. This will dramatically improve your ability to listen more effectively. Read on so you can begin to identify, plan and practise skills to improve your listening effectiveness.

Listening skill development is an ongoing process. Good listening is a key to success in any business environment. Discovering your attitude about listening is an important first step towards successful listening. Attitudes determine our behaviour. To discover your listening atitudes, complete the following exercises. If a statement describes your listening attitude or behaviour accurately, tick 'Yes', if not, tick 'No'. Be hard on yourself.

Listening attitudes and behaviour

	Yes	*No*
1. I am interested in many subjects and do not knowingly tune out dry-sounding information.	☐	☐
2. I listen carefully for a speaker's main ideas and supporting points.	☐	☐
3. I take notes during meetings to record key points.	☐	☐
4. I am not easily distracted.	☐	☐
5. I keep my emotions under control.	☐	☐
6. I concentrate carefully and do not fake attention.	☐	☐
7. I wait for the speaker to finish before finally evaluating the message.	☐	☐
8. I respond appropriately with a smile, a nod, or a word of acknowledgement, as a speaker is talking.	☐	☐
9. I am aware of mannerisms that may distract a speaker and keep mine under control.	☐	☐
10. I understand my biases and control them when I am listening.	☐	☐
11. I refrain from constant interruption.	☐	☐
12. I value eye contact and maintain it most of the time.	☐	☐
13. I often restate or paraphrase what the speaker said to make sure I have the correct meaning.	☐	☐
14. I listen for the speaker's emotional meaning as well as subject matter content.	☐	☐
15. I ask questions for clarification.	☐	☐
16. I do not finish other people's sentences unless asked to do so.	☐	☐

		Yes	No
17.	When listening on the telephone one hand is kept free to take notes.	☐	☐
18.	I attempt to set aside my ego and focus on the speaker rather than on myself.	☐	☐
19.	I am careful to judge the message rather than the speaker.	☐	☐
20.	I am a patient listener most of the time.	☐	☐

The following scale will help you to interpret your present listening skill level based on your current atitudes and behaviour patterns.

1–5 'No' answers	You are an excellent listener. Keep it up!
6–10 'No' answers	You are a good listener, but can improve.
11–15 'No' answers	Through practice you can become a much more effective listener in your business and personal relationships.
16–20 'No' answers	Listen harder!

Personal listening inventory

The personal listening inventory on the facing page will help you to rate yourself as a listener. An interpretation of results follows this inventory. When you have completed it you will have a better insight into:

How much time you spend listening;
How you rate yourself as a listener;
How you think others rate you as a listener;
How you rate others as listeners.

1. On a scale of 1–10 (with 10 being highest), how committed are you to improving your listening?____
2. On average, what percentage of each business day do you spend listening? ____
3. On a scale of 1–10 (with 10 being the highest), how would you rate yourself as a listener? ____
4. On a scale of 1–10, how would you rate the best listener you know? ____
5. On a scale of 1–10, how would you rate the worst listener you know? ____
6. On a scale of 1–10 (with 10 being highest), how would the following people (where appropriate) rate you as a listener?

   Manager ____   Spouse/Lover ____
   Subordinate ____   Child(ren) ____
   Close colleague ____   Best friend ____

Now for the author's interpretation of the personal listening inventory.

Personal listening inventory – author responses
The following interpretation of the personal listening inventory will help you to compare your results with those of others.

1. We need to become committed to becoming better listeners, because *listening is hard work*. It requires patience, persistence and a plan for improvement. Casual involvement and genuine commitment are not the same thing. Suppose you had bacon and eggs for breakfast. The chicken was involved in the meal, but the pig was committed. What is you commitment to your listening improvement?
2. According to experts we spend approximately 80 per cent of each business day communicating. Of our time, 45 per cent is spent listening, 30 per cent speaking, 16 per cent reading and 9 per cent writing. A manager may spend up

to 60 per cent of each business day listening.

3. Most people listen at about 50 per cent efficiency during the first part of an oral communication. In other words, if tested immediately on what they just heard they would accurately remember 50 per cent. However, the efficiency rate drops quickly after the initial statements. Most people average a 25 per cent efficiency rate overall.

4. Best listeners are usually rated as 8, 9 or 10. This is higher than most individuals rate themselves. The best listeners are often mentors, role models or professional counsellors.

5. Worst listeners are usually rated at 0–4. This score is much lower than most people rate themselves. 'Worst listeners' are often related to us, probably because we save our worst behaviour for the people closest to us.

6. It is not unusual to discover that our best friends rate us highest and our family lowest. Subordinates and colleagues rank us about the same as we rank ourselves. Bosses usually rank us higher than we rank ourselves because we listen (or pretend to) better to them than to others. In other words, we are more attentive when there is a direct reward or penalty.

Your listening qualities: an awareness exercise

1. List five of your best listening qualities, such as, patience, good eye contact, not jumping to conclusions, asking for clarification, etc, and rank them 1 – 5, with 1 being your best quality.
    1.
    2.
    3.
    4.
    5.

2. List three listening qualities that you don't have now but would like.
    1.
    2.
    3.

3. List five of your worst listening qualities, such as impatience, poor eye contact, jumping to conclusions, not asking for clarification, etc, and rank them, with 1 being the worst.

    1.
    2.
    3.
    4.
    5.   .

4. List three listening qualities of poor listeners you know that you would like to avoid. Make a commitment to be more patient with those people, and not fall into those habits yourself.

    1.
    2.
    3.

Now read on to see how to eliminate bad listening habits and replace them with good ones.

How to stop bad listening habits

1. Catch yourself in the act
Recognition is the first step for preventive maintenance. By listing the listening habits you want to eliminate in the previous section, you should be more readily able to recognise them. By monitoring your listening behaviour you can catch yourself when you fall into undesirable behaviour, then take steps towards positive change.

2. Fight the habit
Don't tolerate what you want to eliminate from your listening style. Stop it. Drop it. Change your ways! Don't wait until next time to do things differently. Admit your fault (ie, 'I just interrupted you. I'm sorry, please go on with what you were saying.') This is a way of catching yourself in the act and acknowledging your bad habit.

3. Substitute the old habit with a new habit

Memorise the list of new habits you want to develop. If you are chronically impatient, find a way to learn patience. For example, think about how you appreciate other people's patience when you are trying to explain something, then act the way you were treated. Visualise yourself as being patient (or not interrupting, or listening without daydreaming, etc). Look for the value in the new behaviour you select and trust yourself to do it.

4. Acknowledge your success

When you successfully substitute improved listening behaviour, give yourself a reward – a pat on the back. Put £5 towards a holiday fund, or a star in your listening diary. Say to yourself, 'I did it!' Tell someone to see if they praise you; or better yet, tell someone you know *will* praise you.

CHAPTER 5
Ten Tips for Tip-Top Listening

Listening is both behaviour and a skill. Our behaviour is the evidence of our ability to apply a skill. To improve our listening skills we need to consciously practise the ten tips in this chapter. A good driver does more than simply avoid accidents and a good listeners does more than simply pay attention.

The following tips will help you to 'listen louder'. Consciously select those you wish to work on and then establish a list of listening priorities. A personal action plan is given on page 59. Here you will be asked to list the listening skills you want to improve, developing some goals and establishing a plan to meet those goals.

Because business is a place where you need to listen most of the time, you will have plenty of opportunity to practise. Mentally condition yourself to make every encounter, from your first phone call to the last meeting of your business day, an opportunity to practise improved listening. Be practical and select the tips that will help you the most.

Tip 1: Take notes

Good listeners are note-takers. They realise that minds are imprecise and memory is imperfect. Note-taking will help you to identify unorganised speakers, locate the key points and identify supporting data. The following suggestions can help you to improve your note-taking skills.

Be prepared. Carry a small note pad and a pen at all times. (Some people prefer to carry a small tape recorder.) Use the pad or tape recorder regularly to record thoughts or ideas you want to remember. Note the source (speaker), situation, and time. (In selected situations you should ask permission before taking notes or recording what is said. Use good judgement.)

Get it down. Don't take time to be overly neat. If necessary you can copy your notes later. Write clearly enough to remember what you wrote and why you wrote it.

Don't try to write everything. Avoid complete sentences. Write nouns that create visual pictures. Use active verbs. Develop and use your own shorthand including symbols, pictures, punctuation and abbreviations (ie, Suzie Hilgeman, Lnch w/ HP client, Fri. 11.30 @ JoJo's).

Tip 2: Listen now, report later

You can improve your listening significantly by planning to report what you heard to someone later. (Taking notes will increase your effectiveness even more.) Think of a colleague or friend who would benefit from or enjoy the information you're listening to and plan to tell him or her what you've heard. Your listening then takes on the added dimension of a rehearsal.

Case study

Ray is the sales manager for a large manufacturing company in Dundee. Recently his company received some customer complaints about one of their important new products. Ray quickly acted to set up a hotline and requested that all complaints be referred to him immediately.

By listening carefully to complaints from the customers, Ray was able to identify three specific manufacturing problems. He did not know personally how to solve the problems, but by responding quickly and listening carefully he assured his customers that action would be taken and the problems would be resolved. Because Ray showed concern by listening carefully, the customers agreed to support the product until a solution was found. They approved the time Ray estimated would be required to make the changes.

Ray took the information he received through listening to

the manufacturing manager and carefully reported his findings. The manufacturing manager was upset by the magnitude of the problems, but grateful for the feedback. The manufacturing manager and his staff were able to make several adjustments to the manufacturing process which not only solved the problem, but actually improved his product.

How would you rate Ray as a listener?
___ Excellent ___ Good ___ Average ___ Fair ___ Poor

Tip 3: Learn to want to listen

To be good listeners we must be willing to give up a preoccupation with ourselves. Simply put, we must learn to *want* to listen. The following memory device describes the skills and attitudes we need to ensure our listening success:

To be a good listener, use your DISC drive

D = Desire	From a desire to listen comes commitment. A committed athlete does not play half of each game. We must *want* to learn to listen to be a truly effective communicator.
I = Interest	According to G K Chesterton, there is no such thing as an uninteresting topic, there are just uninterested people. We must learn to develop an interest in either the person and/or the topic in order to be a good listener.
S =Self-discipline	We must learn self-discipline in order to eliminate distractions, understand the speaker's key points, overcome boredom, interpret voice inflection and tone, understand non-verbal cues and comprehend the main ideas. Next time you are in a listening situation, pay attention to how well you control your listening habits. Monitoring your listening behaviour is essential for taking positive action later.

C = Concentration Concentration is focused mental energy. Think of concentration as your salary. If you are like most people, your salary is a limited resource that must be spent carefully. If you do not concentrate on your income versus your expenses you will soon be in trouble. Lack of concentration in listening is no different.

As products of the 'TV generation' most of us concentrate intensely for only a few moments at a time. Try flipping on the TV and see how long you can concentrate before your mind wanders. If you are like most people you will probably focus for only a few seconds.

LISTENING LAB

Complete the following exercise to identify reasons you do not always concentrate.

Concentration checklist
Rate the following which apply to you using a scale from 0 to 3, with 0 being no problems; 1 being a minor problem; 2 being somewhat of a problem; and 3 being a major problem. Total your score and compare it with the box at the end of the exercise.

1. I'm in a hurry ____
2. I become distracted by what is going on around me ____
3. I'm self-conscious ____
4. I'm bored ____
5. I'm thinking about what I'm going to say next ____
6. I'm in surroundings that are 'out of my comfort zone'____
7. I already know what the speaker is going to say ____
8. I'm used to having things repeated ____
9. I'm on mental overload most of the time ____
10. I'm not responsible for the information given ____
11. I'm tired ____

12. I'm confused by the topic or the speaker ____
13. I'm daydreaming ____

0–5	You have excellent concentration skills.
6–10	This book should help to improve your concentration skills.
11 or more	You need to put into practice a specific action plan to improve your concentration skills.

To improve your concentration develop an opportunistic attitude. Ask yourself:

• What's in it for me?
• What can I learn or pass on to a colleague?
• How can I use this information?

Concentration improves when you develop mental pictures of what the speaker is saying. If Joe phones to say that he will have the Wilson report on your desk by 2.30 pm on Friday, visualise Joe placing the report on your desk. Notice how Joe is dressed. Image the word WILSON in bold letters on the cover of the report. See in your mind a clock that reads 2.30 pm next to your desk calendar turned to Friday. By visualising what you want to remember, you create 'dwell time' for your mind to encode the information into your long-term memory.

To be a good listener we must use our DISC drive. Just as a disc drive services the computer, so our personal DISC drive controls our attitudes, skills and behaviour in listening situations.

Tip 4: Be present

Like it or not, we always choose whether and how well we are going to listen. When we choose not to listen, our minds are on vacation and we do not interpret, evaluate or respond appropriately to the speaker and the message. Only when we choose to 'be present' are we focused on the speaker and the message.

Our number one alternative to being present is daydreaming. Daydreaming is a comfortable private escape. It normally doen't disturb anyone and often others don't realise we're doing it. Daydreaming is what we elect to do when we choose not to be presnt.

Daydreaming is the single greatest barrier to active listening. To be present and listen effectively, we must recognise our mental vacations, put them aside and bring ourselves back to the subject in hand. The following exercise will help you to recognise your DQ (Daydream Quotient) and suggest steps to take in order to be present in your listening.

LISTENING LAB

Your daydream quotient
In the following exercise take a piece of paper and jot down any time you daydream as you read the rest of this book. If your mind wanders, jot down where it went and what you were thinking about, then quickly return your attention to your reading. Reading and listening are similar in that they both allow opportunities for daydreaming. Notice any tendency you may have to let your mind wander as you read, and write it down. When you complete *A Practical Guide to Effective Listening*, review your DQ to see if there are repeated subjects or patterns in your daydreams. If so, they may be matters for conscious attention and action.

We all daydream
We all daydream. Many of us as much as 50 per cent of the time. Next time you are in a listening situation check your DQ to notice how often you mentally wander off while the speaker is talking. If you 'wander' at least once per minute, the chances are you need more concentration and self-discipline in your listening.

Effective listeners focus on the speaker and listen hard for the content of the message. They avoid the embarrassment of being caught daydreaming. While we are never tested on our daydreams, we can, at any time, be tested on the content of the message.

Tip 5: Anticipate excellence

In the film *Brain Power*, John Houseman presented a powerful story about a group of normal men who checked themselves into a mental hospital. Each had invented a different story explaining why he was crazy. All studied and displayed classic textbook symptoms of mental illness. Once inside the hospital they began to tell the truth, but no one believed them. Only after great difficulty and with outside verification were they released from the hospital.

Expectations play a powerful role in our lives. How often have we avoided a colleague because we didn't want to spend time listening to small talk. Other times we may have made up an excuse to miss a speaker we expected to find boring.

By giving others a chance to speak intelligently and by anticipating excellence from them, we can help them to become successful. As humans we have a deep and unending need to be heard and understood. When we set aside our needs and truly listen, people will drop their pretences and speak to us in a more mature and connected manner.

Listeners can help speakers by

- Asking questions
- Showing interest
- Expressing concern
- Paying attention.

People do their best when they know someone is listening.

The pioneer's story

The following story is about some pioneers in covered wagons who crossed into the new Oregon Territory. They stopped to rest at a small settlement and the wagon master spoke to an old man sunning himself in front of the general store.

'Say Old Timer, what kind of people have settled out here?'

'What kind of people were they where you came from?' asked the old man.

'Well they were mean, full of mischief and small minded. that's why we left,' said the wagon master.

'Sorry to say, young feller, but that's the kind of folks you'll find out here,' replied the old man.

Later in the week another team of wagons pulled into town for supplies. This wagon master also stopped in front of the general store and saw the same old man sunning on the steps.

'Say, Old Timer, what kind of people have settled out here?'

'What kind of people were they where you came from?', asked the old man again.

'The people we left behind were kind, decent people and they were generous. When we left they gave us supplies and helped us load our wagons. We all miss them very much', sighed the wagon master.

'Well, my friend, you've come to the right place, because those are the kind of people you're going to find out there', replied the old man with a kindly smile.

We get what we expect! Anticipate excellence, and it will happen a lot more often than if we assume otherwise.

Tip 6: Become a 'whole body' listener

To be effective listeners we must involve our whole body. Not only are our ears tuned in, but so are our eyes, our mind (the intellect), our bodies and hearts. Good listeners give both non-verbal and verbal signals that they are listening.

A 'whole body' listener listens actively by:

- Conveying a positive, encouraging attitude
- Sitting in an attentive posture (facing the speaker)
- Remaining alert, but comfortable.
- Nodding in acknowledgement of the speaker's words
- Making good eye contact
- Ignoring or eliminating distractions
- Tuning in to the speaker's feelings
- Looking like a listener.

If you are in total rapport you will naturally match the

speaker's physical movements, tone of voice, vocabulary and breathing patterns. Good listeners are in sensory balance with the speaker.

According to Albert Mehrabian, an expert in human behaviour, our communication is 55 per cent non-verbal, 38 per cent inflection and tone and only 7 per cent words.

If Mehrabian is correct, then most of the message is *seen* and *sensed*, and the words are far less important than the non-verbal cues and tone of voice.

Think about your personal mannerisms and behaviour. Do you have any of the following habits that would distract or confuse a speaker?

- Fidgeting
- Blinking
- Biting your lip
- Frowning deeply
- Playing with your hair, tie or jewellery
- Looking at your watch
- etc.

Stop for a moment and think about these habits. Would they distract you if you were the one speaking? If your answer is yes, you need to find a way to modify your behaviour. Try the suggestions in the following section.

LISTENING LAB

1. Body check exercise
Briefly describe your non-verbal listening responses with two people you know. Make one a person you enjoy being with and the other a person you don't. Are your responses different? If so, how? If you want to change any of your non-verbal responses to either person use the *Change* line to state your improvement goal.

Person 1 _____

Response	Description	Change

Posture
Eye contact
Facial Expression
Mannerisms
General Attitude
Voice (verbal response)

Person 2 _____

Response	Description	Change

Posture
Eye contact
Facial Expression
Mannerisms
General Attitude
Voice (verbal response)

2. Non-verbal encouragement exercise
List five things you can do non-verbally to encourage a speaker.

    1.
    2.
    3.
    4.
    5.

Tip 7: Build rapport by pacing the speaker

Pacing is a method listeners use to build rapport with a speaker by imitating or mirroring his or her behaviour. This involves gestures, breathing, voice rate, vocabulary, favourite phrases and facial expressions. Of course, if we imitate too closely we will be accused of mimicking, and our attempts to build rapport will be lost. When pacing, a good listener focuses on who the speaker is and what he or she is saying. The listener then makes a conscious effort to overcome the differences between them. The sooner the speaker and listener find common ground, the sooner they can communicate at a comfortable level. From that point, their opportunity for mutual understanding will be greater.

As a listener, you can pace a speaker in any of the following ways:

1. *Match your voice rate to theirs.* Speed up or slow down as necessary.
2. *Change your voice volume to match theirs.*
3. *Notice and use some of the same words and phrases as the speaker.*
4. *Approximate the speaker's gestures.* Sit forward or back, hands on or off the desk, etc. (Do not be too obvious or you will be noticed. *Approximate* the gestures.)
5. *Breathe at about the same rate, without being too obvious.* (If the speaker is a Type A and breathes very fast be careful not to hyperventilate.)

Cheryl's story

Cheryl was preparing to give a technical speech before a large, important audience. She arrived early at the meeting room to test her slides and adapt to the circumstances of the room. When she turned on the hired projector, the bulb in the machine suddenly burned out. Cheryl looked in the projector case but could not find a replacement. Frantically, she searched the building for a maintenance person. She found the maintenance supervisor on the next floor, ambling slowly down the hall. She rushed to the supervisor, explaining her dilemma in a rapid staccato voice which displayed an obvious urgency.

Bill, the supervisor, was low keyed. While Cheryl churned like a buzz saw, Bill spoke no faster than a snail, on valium. Cheryl felt she could count to ten between each of Bill's words. 'I'd - like - to - help - you, - but - I - don't - have - a - key - to - the - supply - cupboard,' Bill said in a low slow, patient monotone. Cheryl continued to buzz and Bill continued to dawdle for several more minutes.

Suddenly, Cheryl remembered something she had read about pacing a speaker and she decided to give it a try. Gradually, she began to slow her speech to match Bill's rate. It was painful for Cheryl to talk so slowly, but Bill became more responsive and more helpful as she became less frantic.

Within minutes Bill remembered someone who had a key and volunteered to find the bulb she needed. Cheryl couldn't be sure the pacing made the difference, but within 15 minutes she had the replacement bulb. Bill flashed her a big slow smile as he handed her the bulb, along with a spare, in case the replacement burned out. Cheryl thanked him s-l-o-w-l-y, and smiled back. She had found a new friend.

Brian's story
Brian was an independent sales representative for a refrigeration company in Scotland. Because of the nature of his territory Brian made most of his contacts by telephone. He had heard of pacing from a friend and decided to try it in his telephone selling.

When he phoned potential customers he listened very carefully to *what* they said and *how* they said it. Then as he spoke, he paced their voices, speed, inflection and vocabulary. With no variables in his experiment other than pacing, Brian was able to increase his refrigeration equipment sales by 30 per cent over the previous quarter.

LISTENING LAB

Pacing the speaker
To develop an ability to pace effectively, follow these guidelines in the suggested sequence:

1. Practise pacing with a friend. Tell him or her what you are doing first. Have your friend tell you a funny story or describe an interesting place to visit and use varied gestures and facial expressions. Mirror each action and expression to get the feeling for the pacing activity.

Afterwards, discuss how successful you were and solicit suggestions for improvement.
2. Next, practise pacing on a friend or family member in a no-risk situation. Try to remain undetected.
3. Finally, practise on a colleague, choosing one or two characteristics to mirror. Be natural and sincere. As you pace and observe, exhibit an attitude of wanting to build rapport.

Rapport is the ultimate tool in producing positive results with others. In business, dealing effectively with people is essential. Rapport can help us to achieve success, and we build rapport by listening actively and acting on what we learn.

The three keys to pacing
1. Focused observation
2. Complete flexibility
3. Tuned in listening.

Tip 8: Control your emotional 'hot buttons'

Words, issues, situations, and/or personalities trigger us emotionally. When these issues trigger our emotional 'hot buttons' a verbal message will become distorted (either positively or negatively). Because issues are emotional they create barriers to effective listening. When our 'hot buttons' are activated, we tune out, distort or prejudge these emotionally charged messages. The three-step method that follows can help you to identify your listening hot buttons.

LISTENING LAB

Identifying emotional 'hot buttons'

Step 1   Here are some listening situations and phrases that may cause you to be emotional. Tick those that are 'hot buttons' for you as a listener, and add others that strongly affect you, positively or negatively.

——— 'You never/always . . .'
——— Know-all attitudes

—— People who smoke while talking to you
—— 'Shut up!'
—— Bigots
—— Bad grammar
—— 'You never listen.'
—— Pushy individuals
—— Whining
—— 'What you should do is . . .'

Others:

——
——
——

Step 2 Read through the list again and cross out any 'hot button' issues that you are willing to give up; in other words, those you can forget, and not let them bother you any more. Chances are you will not cross many items off your list. This step demonstrates that it is difficult to give up habitual ways of responding to emotional situations.

Step 3 Tick the responses (triggers) on the following list that describe your physical reactions to emotional issues:

—— Heartbeat increases
—— Hands feel sweaty
—— Voice shakes
—— Chest tightens.

Others:

——
——
——

Emotional 'hot buttons' are intense, complex feelings that affect everyone. Each may initiate a different emotional reaction, but our physical responses are similar. If you cannot eliminate your emotional 'hot buttons', the best alternative is to develop acceptable responses. The triggers (listed above) warn you that emotions are taking over. When emotional levels go up, objectively comes down. Problems are never satisfactorily resolved at an emotional level.

To control emotional hot buttons we must identify what triggers us, understand our responses, and develop behaviour which allows us to listen more carefully and objectively.

Ten steps for controlling emotional hot buttons
The following is a list of coping skills for preventive maintenance when your hot button is activated by someone's anger or frustration.

1. *Listen attentively without interrupting.* Take several deep breaths to help you control your physical reactions.
2. *Make a conscious choice about your response.* You can get angry, try to solve the problem, or ignore it. (Trying to solve the problem is the best way to prevent it happening again.)
3. *Acknowledge the other person's feelings.* Make it acceptable for them to feel the way they do.
4. *Ask objective questions for clarification.* Open-ended questions are useful.
5. *Try to see the other person's point of view.* Agree where you can and feed back what you are hearing.
6. *Stick to the subject.* Define your problem and don't let other issues interfere.
7. *Be patient.* Problems don't always have immediate solutions. Be patient with the other person – and yourself.
8. *Express your point of view.* Don't force proof. Present your evidence without backing them into a corner.
9. *Explain why.* A reasonable explanation can often take the sting out of an emotional issue.
10. *Work out a 'win-win' plan.* Make sure your solution is fair and workable for both (or all) of the people involved.

For additional suggestions for changing behaviour refer to 'The joy of small change' on page 17.

LISTENING LAB

Preventive maintenance for emotional 'hot buttons'
In the first column below list three people who affect you emotionally when you listen to them. Next, write down the

hot button issues that activates your reaction. Finally, develop a preventive maintenance plan to contol or modify your emotional reaction.

Person	Hot button	Preventive maintenance plan
1.		
2.		
3.		

Tip 9: Control distractions

A telephone is one of the biggest distractions to listening in a business environment, because unseen, others choose when the phone will ring. If the phone were the only distraction we could probably learn to tolerate it. Every day we must deal with many internal, external, visual and auditory distractions.

To be good listeners, we must control our responses to distractions or they will control us. Distractions affect our ability to listen well because of their *variety, novelty* or *intensity*. External distractions include the telephone, background noise, unfamiliarity with vocabulary, seating, lighting, etc. Internal distractions can be things such as headaches, hunger, fatigue, or a current emotional state, such as anxiety.

Stephanie's story

Stephanie was putting the finishing touches to a major marketing project when a colleague rang to discuss a budget problem. Stephanie automatically grabbed the phone and answered while still assembling binders. Suddenly, she realised her distraction and set the binders aside. She told her colleague politely that she was just finishing a project with a tight deadline and asked if she could return the call in an hour when the project was completed so she could be a better listener. By handling the matter this way, Stephanie avoided being distracted. She let the caller know her desire to give the budget problem her full attention as soon as possible.

Life and work are full of distractions. Part of our professional responsibility is to manage our working environment. Although our working conditions will never be ideal, we can minimise distractions by taking action to improve our listening, which will help to reduce communication failures.

LISTENING LAB

Overcoming distractions

The following statements describe how people might handle various distractions. Tick those items you do well.

☐ *Plan your listening.* Don't attempt to do important business in a restaurant. It's too noisy and you're interrupted frequently. Find a quiet room away from the phone for important meetings. Plan decision-making meetings during your high energy times of the day. Think about possible distractions and plan to avoid as many as you can.

☐ *Don't use distractions as convenient excuses for not listening.* Overcome distractions with extra concentration and determination.

☐ *Identify what is causing a distraction and make adjustments.* Are you too near a noisy copier? (Can you move away from it?) Do you have a headache? (Have you taken an aspirin?) Are you hungry? (Can you eat an apple?) Are the lights too low or too high? (Can they be adjusted?) Is the phone a problem? (Could someone take your calls?) In other words, when you have identified a problem, you are one step closer to fixing it.

☐ *Ignore the distraction.* If you can't do anything about the distraction, tune it out by concentrating harder. Although you know the distraction is there, focus your attention on the speaker. Use self-discipline.

☐ *Call 'time out' when you are too tired to listen.* Audial (hearing) fatigue is caused by constant noise, such as fans humming or the drone of machinery or traffic. Intense concentration or physical exhaustion can also cause 'ear exhaustion'.

Don't be shy about calling a halt when you have had enough noise.

Tip 10: Listening is a gift, give generously

Listening is a skill that anyone can learn, and it is also a gift that anyone can give. It is a gift of a person's time and attention. Listening is an acknowledgement of caring. Honest listening encourages a speaker to be creative and feel more accepted.

According to author, Tom Peters, in his book *In Search of Excellence*, top executives have learned to be excellent listeners. They understand the importance of good listening. The best managers do far more than allow listening to happen. They realise that listening improves effectiveness, accomplishes more, and earns profits.

The gift of listening assumes the speaker has value, dignity and something to offer. We must listen every day in the business world. If in our listening we take the focus off ourselves and encourage the speaker to express his or her ideas we extend a gift that will be repaid many times. Develop a listening attitude. The results are worth it.

CHAPTER 6
Summary: Points to Remember

Summary

1. Why should you (or anyone) listen?
- Work and listening are inseparable.
- Lazy listening is a hidden cost of doing business.
- We listen for our own reasons.
- We can improve listening with desire, motivation and a plan for constructive change.

2. Four key elements of listening: how to be a good listener
- Hear the message. Listen to both verbal and non-verbal information.
- Interpret the message. Good interpretation is a match-up of meaning between the speaker and the listener.
- Evaluate the message. The listener's opinion should be based on *all* available information. Ask questions.
- Respond to the message. Good listening means giving the speaker an appropriate response, verbally and/or non-verbally.

3. Your listening style–a barrier or a bridge?
- Behaviour reflects attitude.
- How we look and act as listeners determines our listening style.

4. How well do you listen?
- Most people aren't good listeners.

- A good listener encourages positive results.
- We listen best when there is a reward or a penalty.
- Personal listening awareness is the key to constructive change.

5. Ten tips for tip-top listening

- Take notes. They aid retention.
- Listen now, report later. Plan to tell someone what you heard; you will remember it better.
- Learn to want to listen. You must have Desire, Interest, Self-discipline and Concentration to be a good listener.
- Be present. Watch the tendency to daydream.
- Anticipate excellence. We get good information more often when we expect it.
- Become a 'whole body' listener. Listen with your ears, your eyes and your heart.
- Build rapport by pacing the speaker. Approximate the speaker's gestures, expressions and voice patterns to create comfortable communication.
- Control your emotional 'hot buttons'. Knowing what makes you react emotionally is your key to preventive maintenance.
- Control distractions. Controlling internal and external distractions helps you to manage your working environment more effectively.
- Give the gift of listening. Listening is a skill, and a gift. Give generously.

Develop a personal action plan

A definition of ACCOUNTABILITY is to be responsible for one's actions.

We all have good intentions. What separates those who are successful from those who are not is how well these good intentions are carried out.

An action plan can convert your good intentions into actions.

The PERSONAL ACTION PLAN on the facing page is a good starting point if you are serious about improving your listening skills.

This action plan can be initiated the next time you are in the role of listener.

Think about the information you have read in this book. Review the exercises, questionnaires and case studies. What did you learn about listening? What did you learn about yourself as a listener? How can you improve your listening skills? Make a commitment to improving your listening in your business and personal life. Design a personal action plan to help you reach your goal.

Personal action plan

The following guide may help you to clarify your goals and outline actions to achieve them. Use them as headings when drawing up your own plan.

1. My current listening skills are effective in the following areas:
2. I need to improve my listening skills in the following areas:
3. I will implement an action plan for listening improvement in the following manner:
    A. My listening goals:
    B. My *plan* for reaching my goals:
    C. My timetable:
    (Refer to page 37 'How to stop bad listening habits' for reinforcement.)
4. The following people will benefit from my improved listening skills:
5. They will benefit in the following ways:

Kathy's story

On Kathy Green's thirtieth birthday she cautiously invited her parents to join the celebration with a few friends. Her mother had baked Kathy's favourite lemon cake and Kathy felt under an obligation. However, she was concerned about the possible reaction of her friends to her parents. Kathy's father was hard-of-hearing and shouted when he spoke. Her mother in turn shouted at her father to tell him what other people were saying. Mrs Green also talked constantly and changed the subject frequently. Almost any response from her listener would catapult Mrs Green on to a new topic. Kathy had long since given up really listening to her mother. Kathy's behaviour was cool and polite, but non-caring.

Kathy attended a company seminar on listening shortly before the celebration. She realised that, although she listened effectively to colleagues, she had developed a habitual 'unhearing' response to her mother.

At her birthday dinner, Kathy began to realise that her mother's behaviour was a bid for attention. Mrs Green was isolated from her husband by his hearing loss and from her only child, by Kathy's imposed distancing. It was true that her mother did not have good communication skills, but Kathy realised that her mother changed the topic in an attempt to be more interesting. The more she was rebuffed, the more she changed the subject.

Kathy made a decision following the night of her birthday to pay more attention to her mother. She focused her listening and developed a genuine interest in what her mother was saying. She worked hard to break old listening patterns and substitute new ones. First she noticed only small changes. Her mother began to stick to the subject longer as Kathy asked patient, relevant questions and listened to the answers. At times Kathy had to guide her mother back to the subject, but she was persistent in her resolve.

After six months Kathy noticed that her mother was calmer and more connected when she spoke. She stopped talking as much and listened with interest as Kathy told her about a recent promotion. True, Mrs Green still shouted at Mr Green, but Kathy stopped hearing it as much. Thanks to a simple increase in listening effectiveness, Kathy was able to renew a loving relationship with her parents.

Kathy learned well the business of listening and we hope you are on your way to doing the same.

Further Reading from Kogan Page

How to Develop Assertiveness: Practical Techniques for Personal Success, Sam R Lloyd

Study Skills Strategies: How to Learn More in Less Time, Uelaine Lengefield

Successful Self-Management: A Sound Approach to Personal Effectiveness, Paul R Timm

Better Management Skills

Effective Performance Appraisals, Robert B Maddux

Effective Presentation Skills, Steve Mandel

The Fifty-Minute Supervisor: A Guide for the Newly Promoted, Elwood N Chapman

How to Develop a Positive Attitude, Elwood N Chapman

Make Every Minute Count: How to Manage Your Time Effectively, Marion E. Haynes

Successful Negotiation, Robert B Maddux

Team Building: An Exercise in Leadership, Robert B Maddux

Effective Meeting Skills, Marion E Haynes.